Instructions: Have students make character puppets.

Instructions: Have students make character puppets.

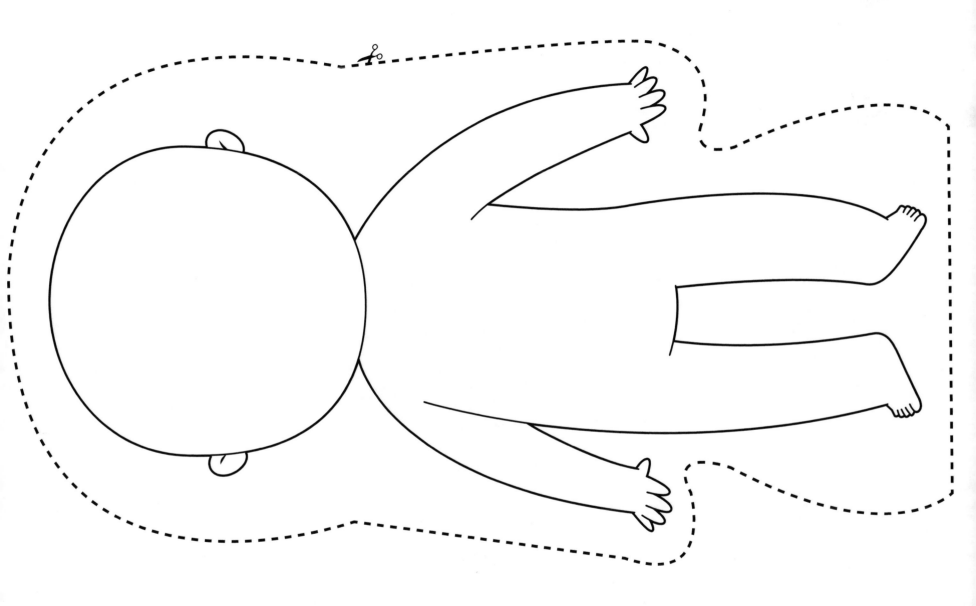

Instructions: Have students make a student puppet.

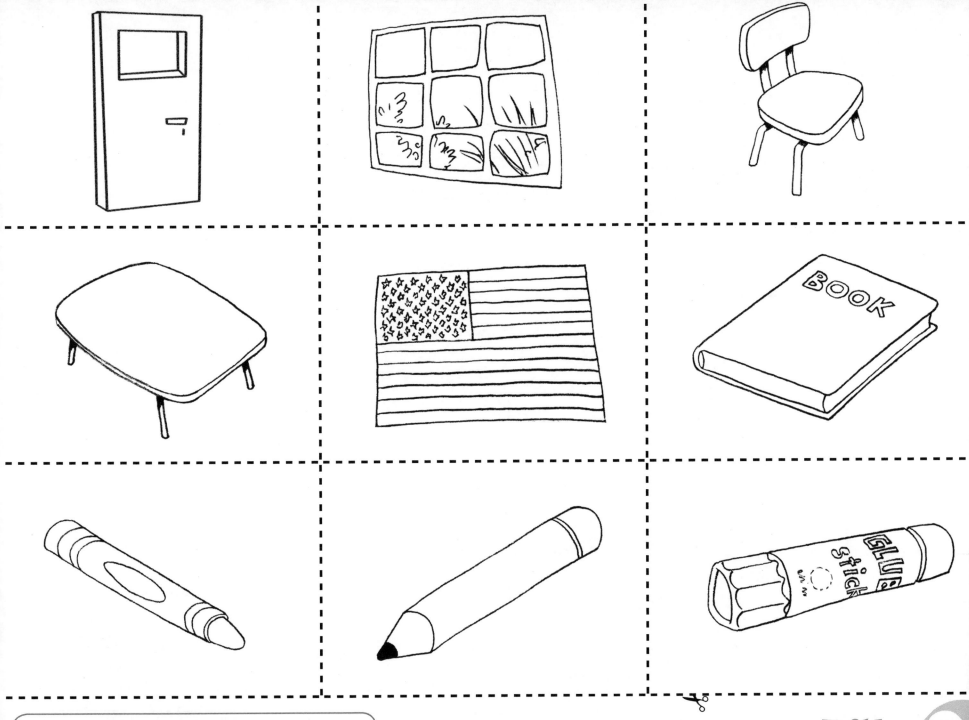

Instructions: Have students color and cut out the game cards.

Unit 1   5

Cut and glue.

Name: _____

GLUE stick

BOOK

Look and circle.

Name: _____

S   M

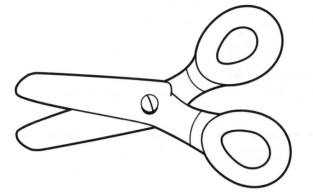

S   M

B   F

B   F

Look and trace.

S s S s S s S s

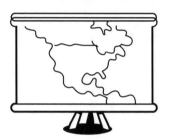

M m M m M m

B b B b B b B b

F f F f F f F f

Trace, cut, and glue.

Name: _____

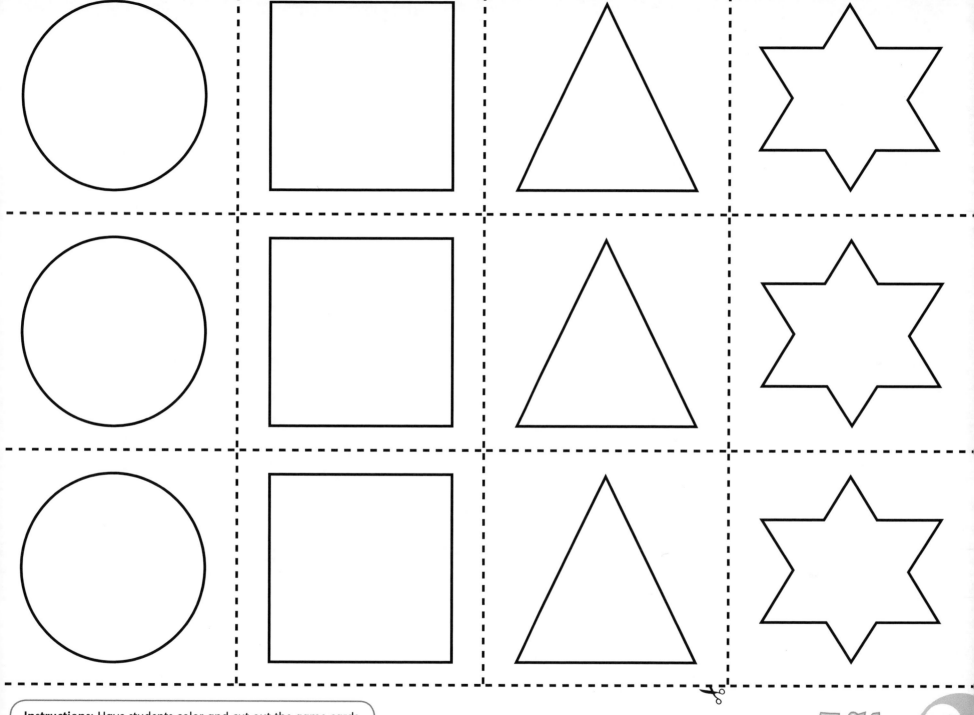

Instructions: Have students color and cut out the game cards.

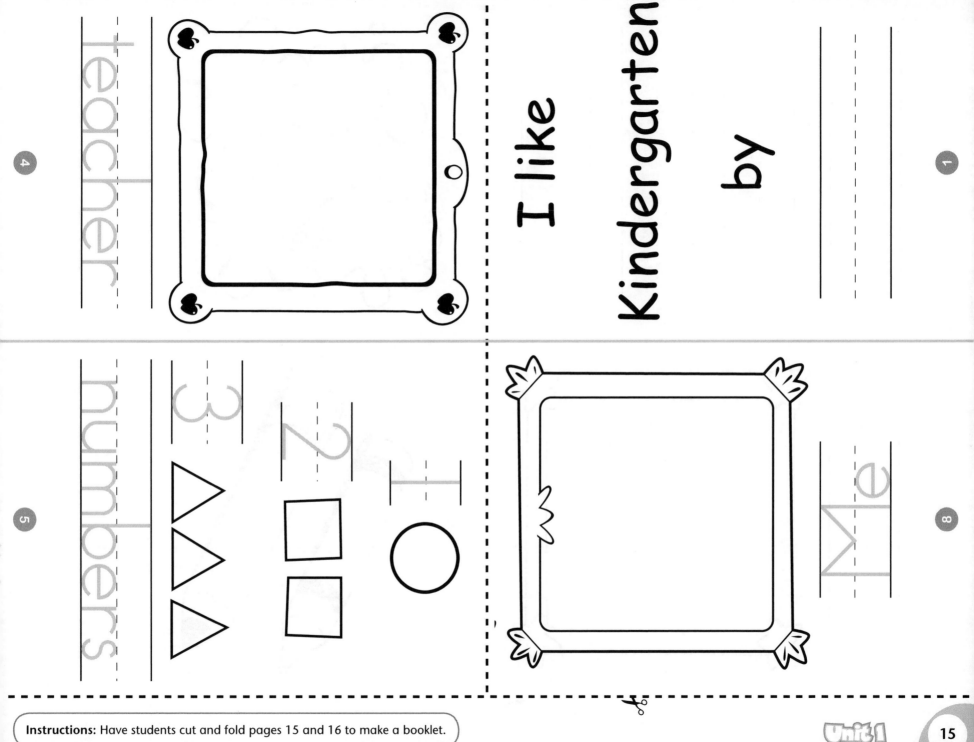

teacher

4

I like
Kindergarten
by

4

numbers

3
2
1

5

Me

8

Instructions: Have students cut and fold pages 15 and 16 to make a booklet.

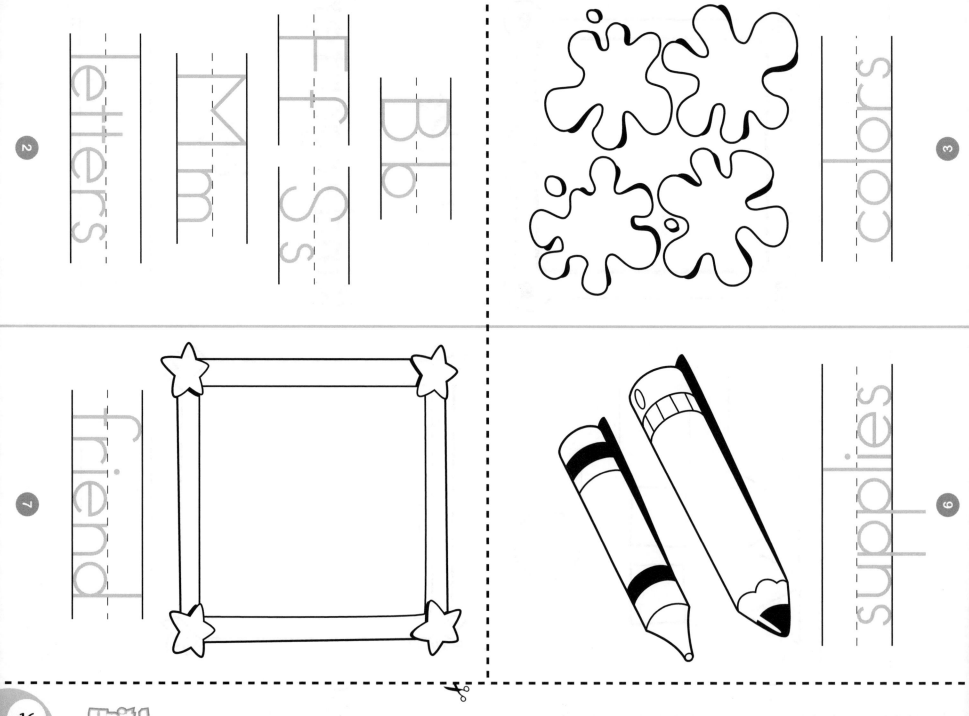

letters

Bb

Ff Ss

Mm

2

colors

3

friend

7

supplies

6

Draw and color.

Name: _____

My Best Friend and I

Circle and mark.

Name: _____

same = ○   different = ✗

This is me.

4

I am a girl.

I am a boy.

3

A Book about
Me

by

1

I am _____
years old.

2

My

His

Her

Unit 2

Instructions: Have students make a paper person and clothes.

A C T D

a c t d

Trace and draw.

I have one

You have two

He is a

She is a

Trace, count, and circle.

Name: _____

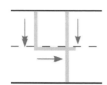      

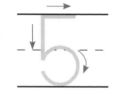     

Unit 2

Draw and write.

Key Words

happy

hungry

mad

sad

scared

tired

Today

_____

- - - - - - - - - - - - - - - - - -

I am _____.

Look and circle.

Name: _____

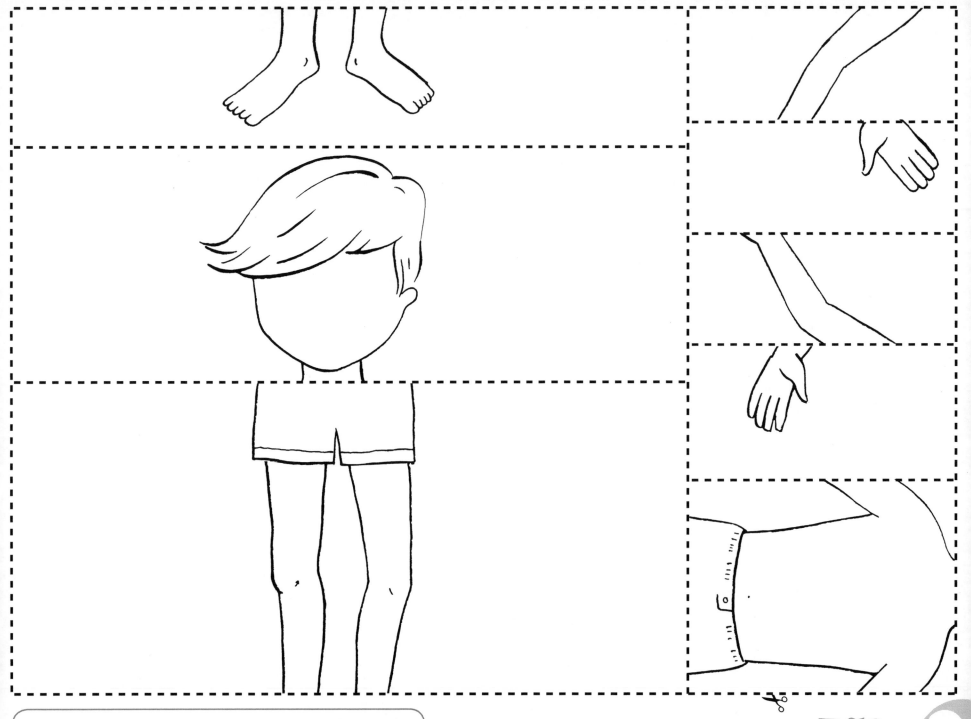

Instructions: Have students cut out the pieces and assemble the puzzle.

Unit 2

31

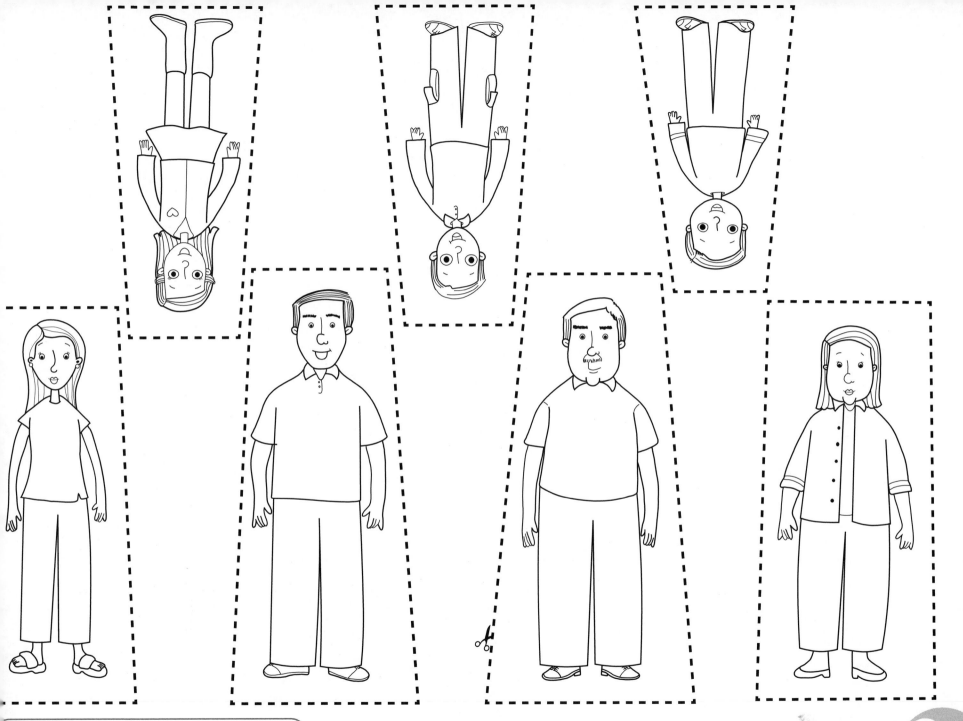

ut and place.

Name: _____

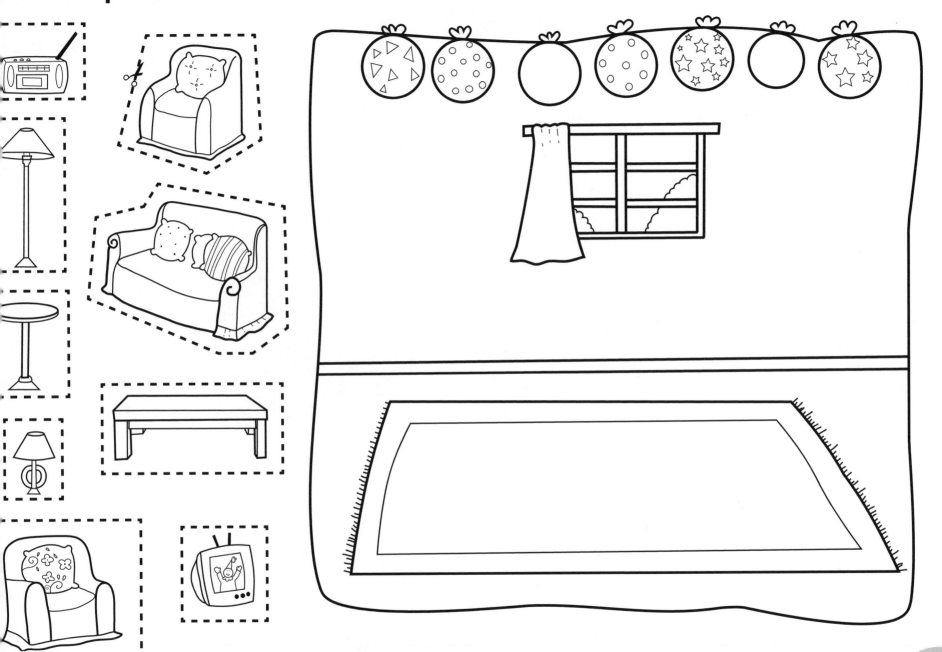

 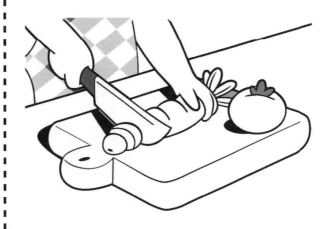 

  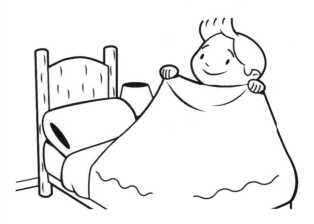

Instructions: Have students color and cut out the game cards.

Unit 3   37

Find and paste.

Name: _____

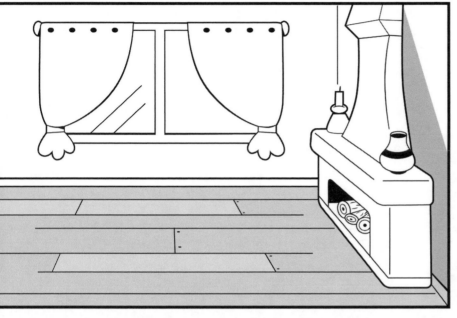

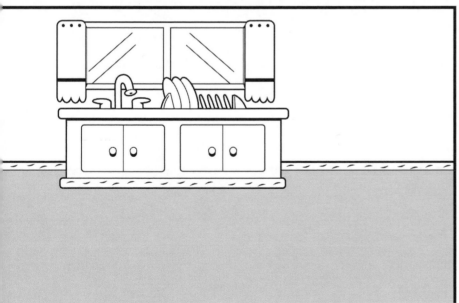

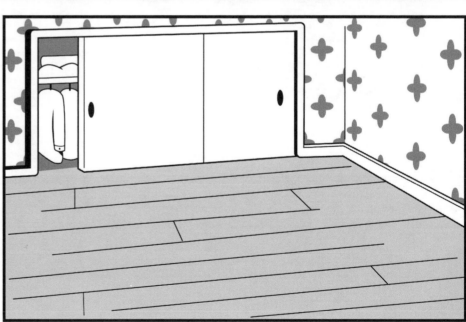

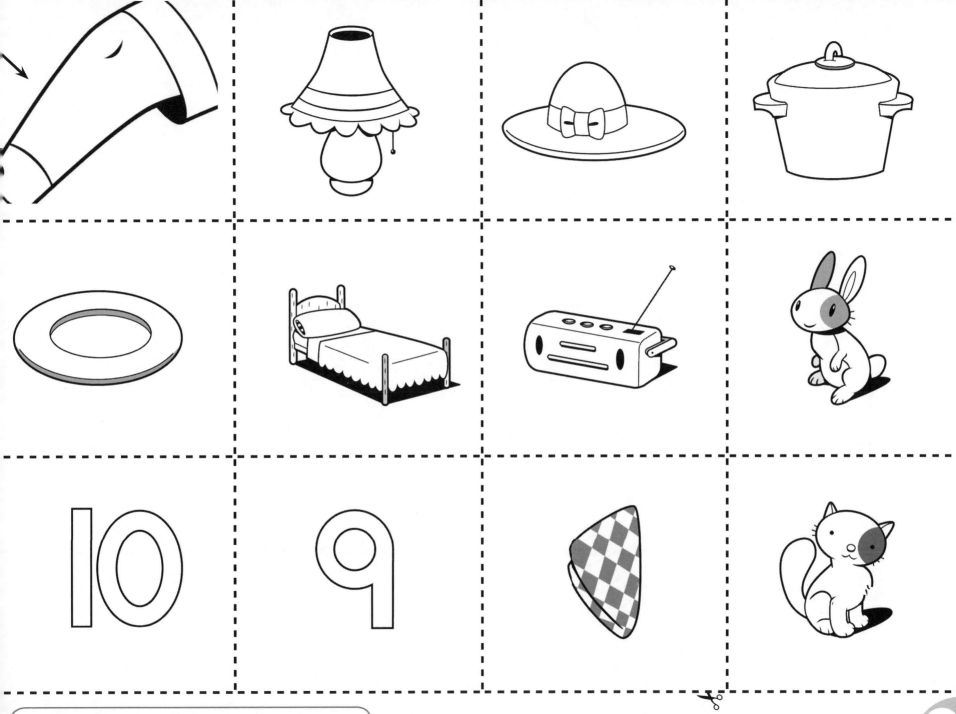

Instructions: Have students color and cut out the game cards.

Unit 3   41

Cut and paste.

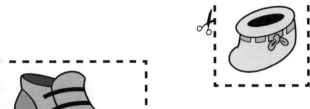

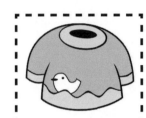

Follow the numbers.

Name: _____

What is she doing?

Find and paste.

Name: _____

paper

plastic

glass

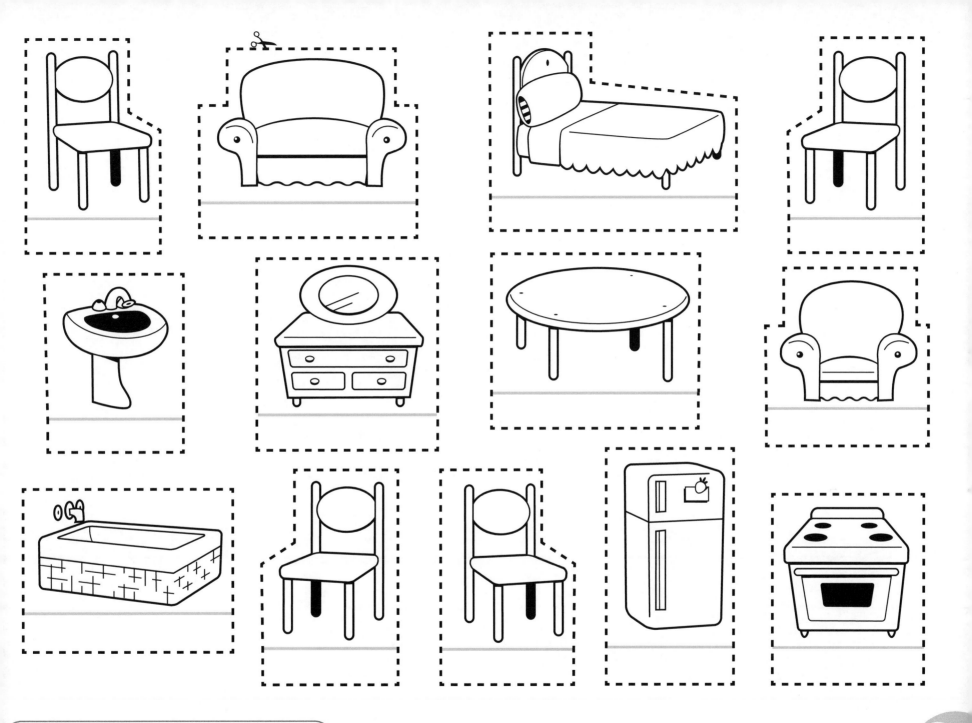

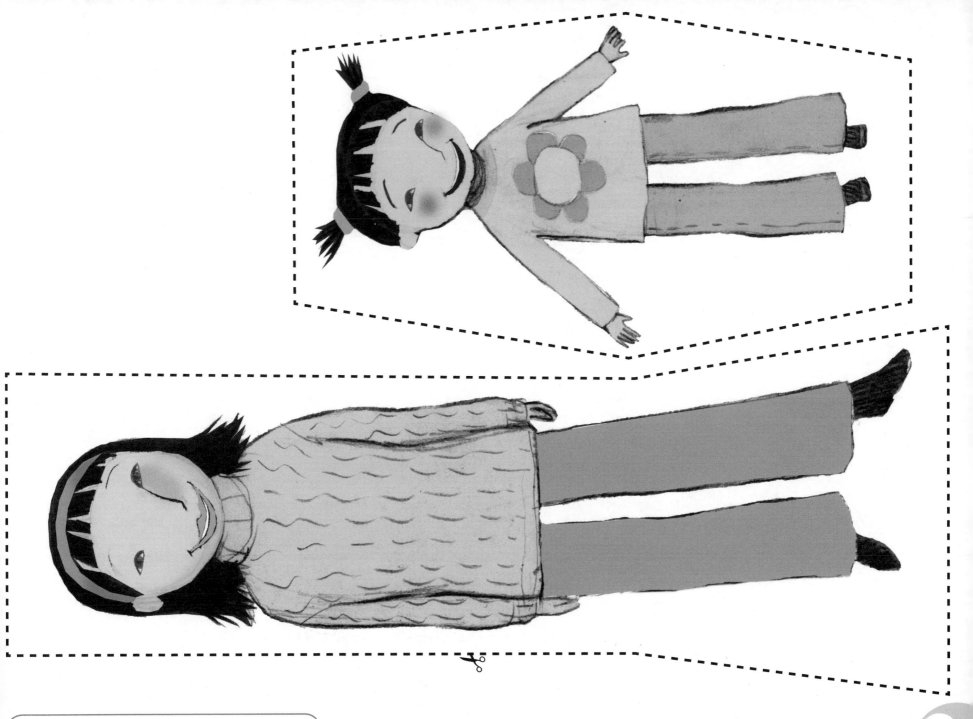

Instructions: Have students make character puppets.

chicken

apple

green beans

cucumbers

carrots

cabbage

zucchini

potatoes

peach

banana

watermelon

orange

Instructions: Have students color and cut out the game cards.

Unit 4   51

Tuesday

4

Breakfast
All Week

by _____

4

Wednesday

5

Saturday

8

Instructions: Have students cut and fold pages 53 and 54 to make a booklet. Have them draw a picture of a breakfast for each day.

Unit 4

53

Sunday

Monday

Friday

Thursday

Color, cut, and paste.

Name: _____

Trace and write.

Name: _____

I i   K k   N n   V v   Z z

A a B b C c D d E e

F f G g H h J j

L l M m O o P p

Q q R r S s T t U u

W w X x Y y

Cut, count, and write.

Name: _____

Sam's Seafood

Total [ ]

Mike's MEAT & CHICKEN

Total [ ]

Pete's Produce

Total [ ]

BEN'S BAKERY

Total [ ]

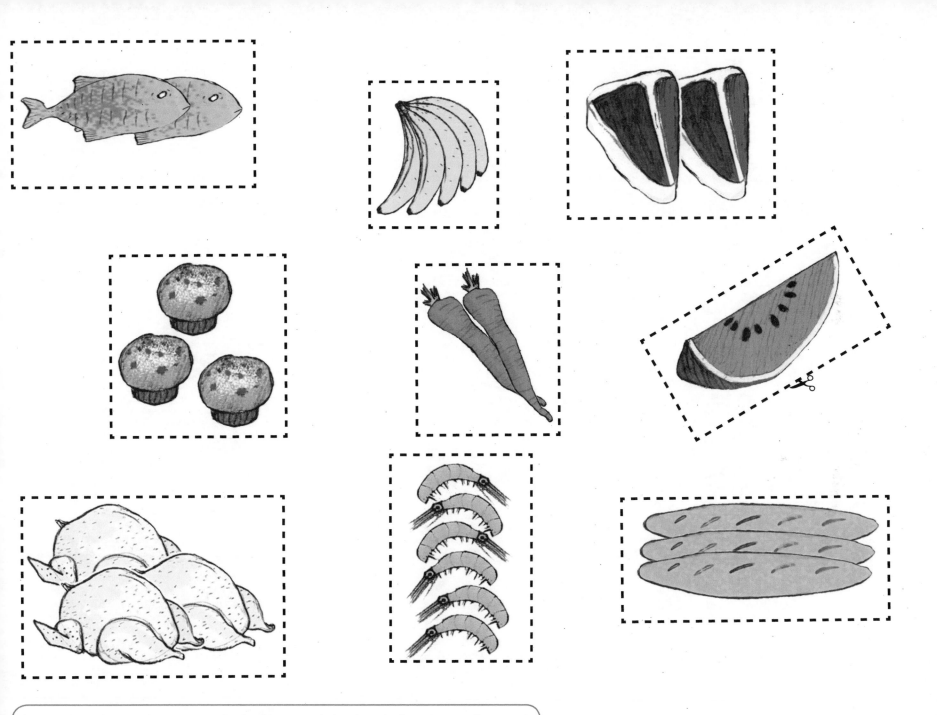

Instructions: Have students cut out the food items and glue them in the corresponding stand on page 58. Then have them count the items in each stand and write the number in the box.

 Unit 4

59

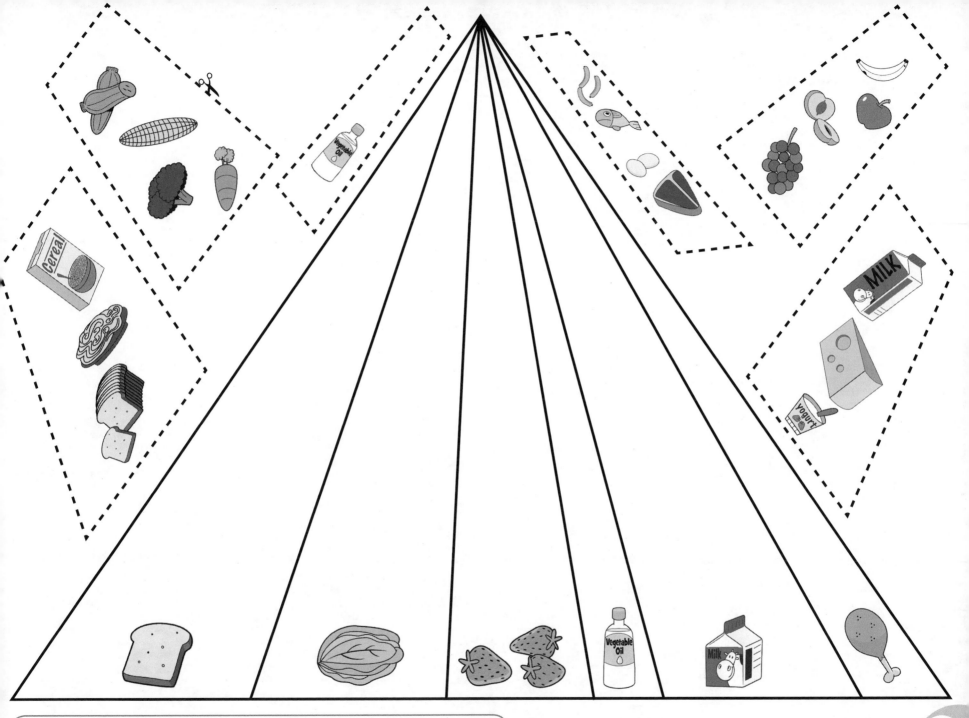

Instruction: Have students cut out the food items and glue them in the correct sections.

Unit 4

61

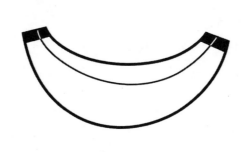

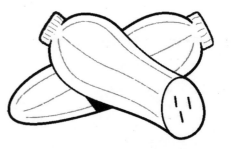

Instructions: Have students color and cut out the game cards.

Unit 4   63

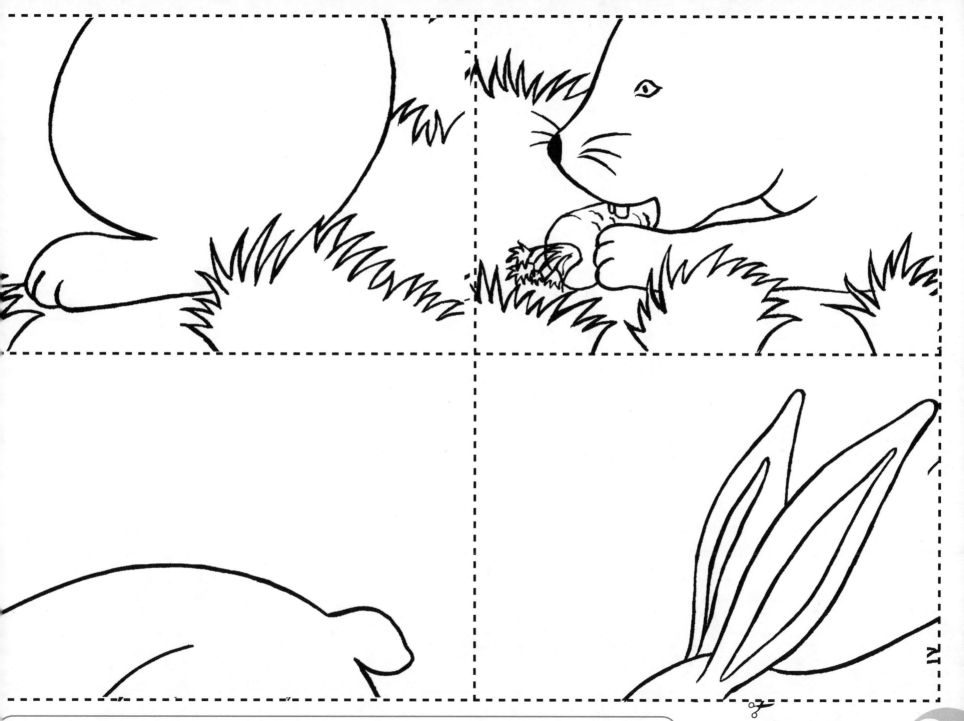

Instructions: Have students cut out and assemble the puzzle on a sheet of paper. Then ask students to color their rabbits.

Look and draw.

Complete and color.

Name: _____

Cut and place.

Name: _____

Cut and paste.

Name: _____

Cut and paste.

Name: _____

c ☐ t

p ☐ g

d ☐ g

m ☐ n

f ☐ sh

fr ☐ g

a a i i o o

Same	
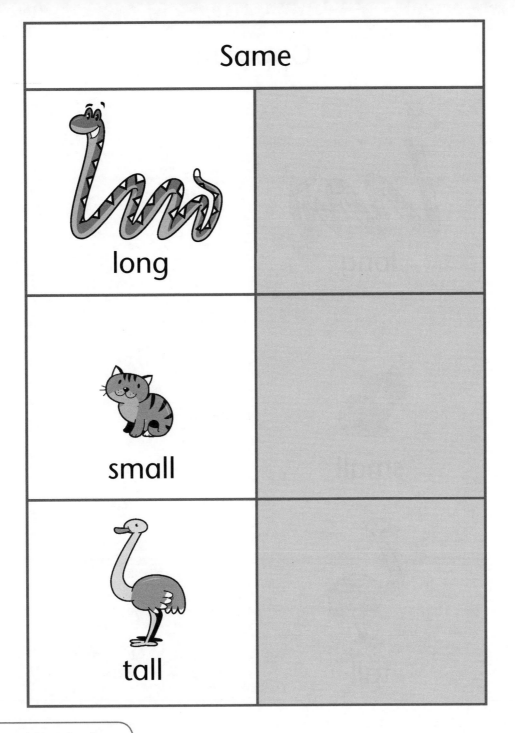 long	
small	
tall	

Opposite	
long	
small	
tall	

Instructions: Have students make Same and Opposite charts.

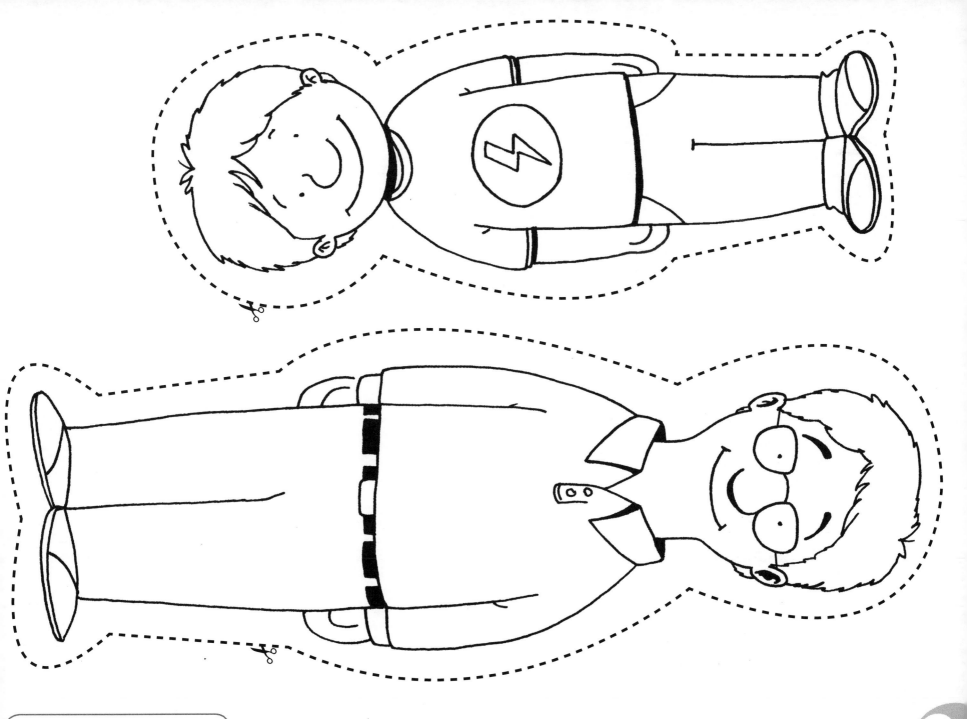

Unit 6

Color, cut, and glue.

Name: _____

Instructions: Color and cut out the cards.

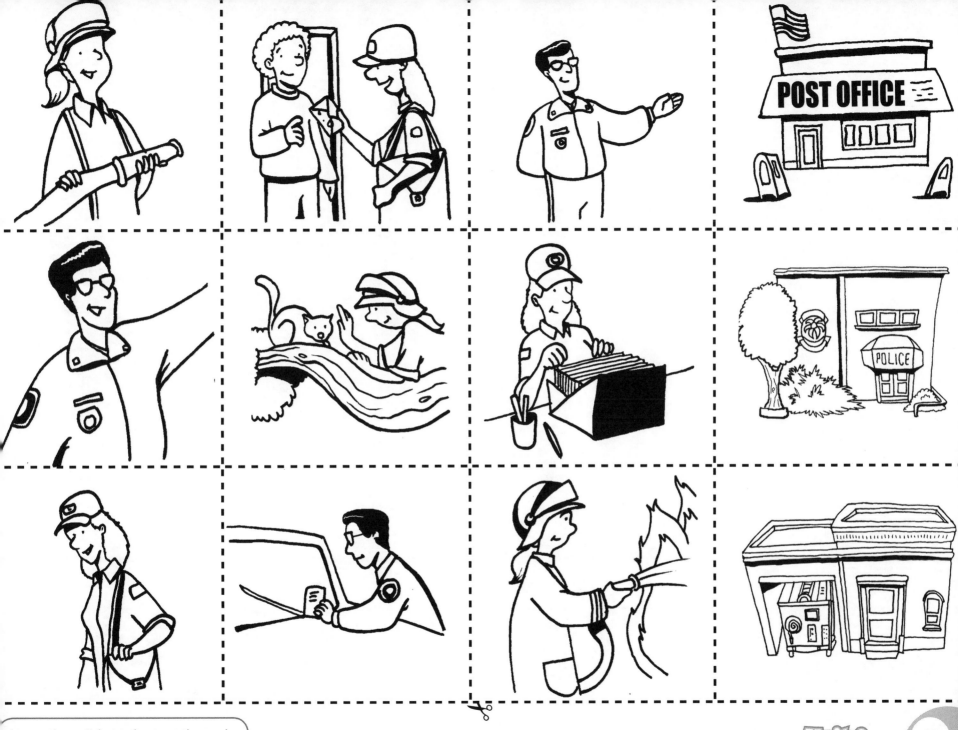

Draw, cut, and complete.

Name: _____

On [ ] , I _____

_____

_____.

✂ -------
Monday

Tuesday

Wednesday

Thursday

Friday

Read and circle.

1	ring	sing	rock	wing
2	cat	book	mat	hat
3	book	cook	took	gum
4	box	house	fox	socks

Trace and complete.

Name: _____

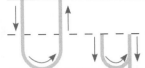

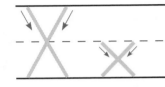

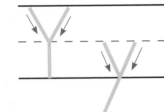

s _____ n

fo _____

to _____

Look and count.

Color the signs.

Name: _____

Old Mother Leary
Left a lantern in the shed.

"There'll be a hot time
In the old town tonight."

Late one night,
When we were
all in bed,

She winked her eye
and said,

And when the cow
kicked it over,

Instructions: Cut out the pictures. Put them in order.

Unit 6   95

4

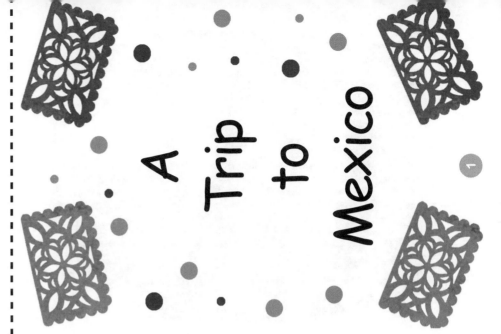

A Trip to Mexico

1

5

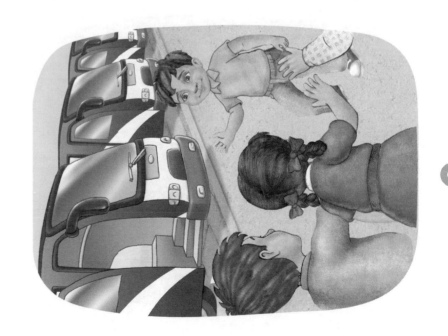

8

2

3

7

6

Unit 7

Instructions: Have students make a story booklet.

ut and paste.

Name: _____

Juan rode … | Juan did not ride …

Cut and paste.

Name: _____

What did Juan eat in Mexico?

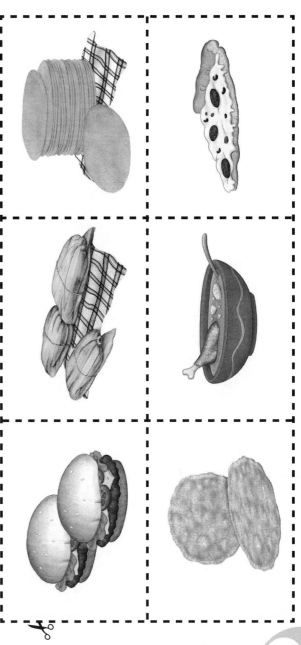

Write, cut, and paste.

Trace, cut, and paste.

Name: _____

I rode on a _____.

I ate _____.

Cut and paste.

Name: _____

2:00

6:30

4:00

Cut, match, and paste.

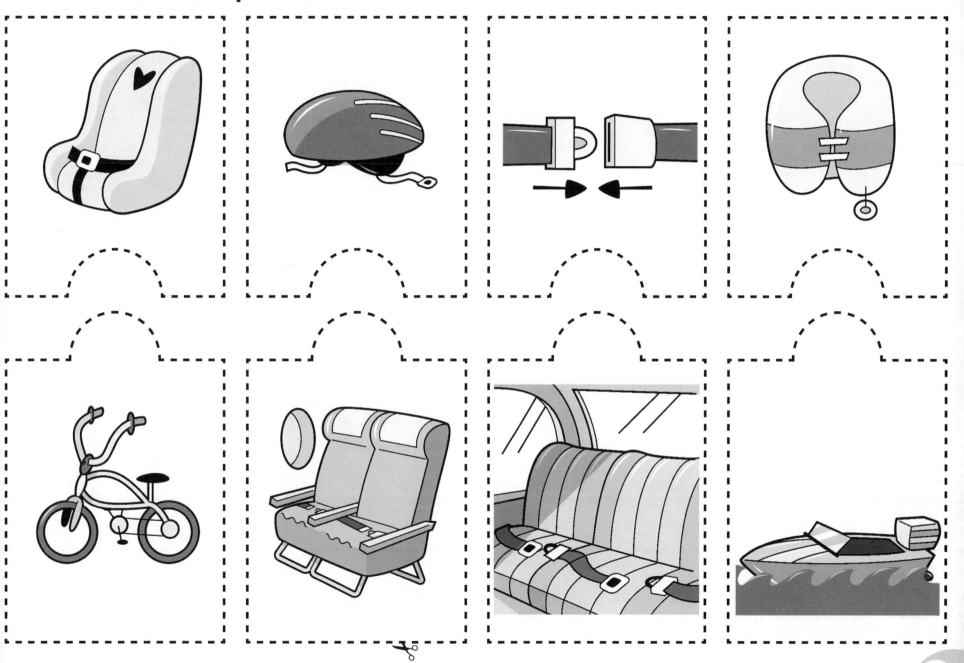

Draw pictures of vehicles.

Name: _____

Air	Land	Water

Circle the differences.

Name: _____

Unit 7

Instructions: Have students circle five things in picture 2 that are different from picture 1.

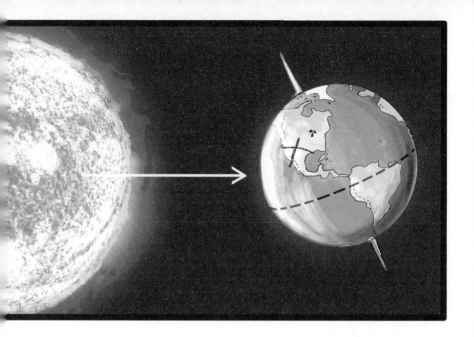

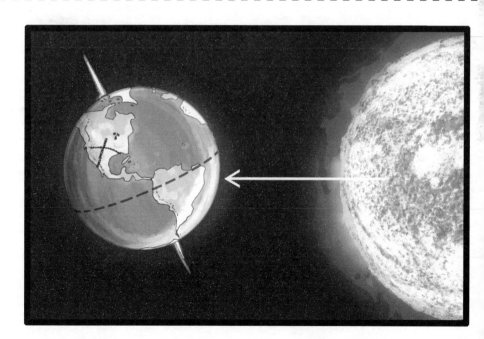

Instructions: Have students cut out the pictures and match.

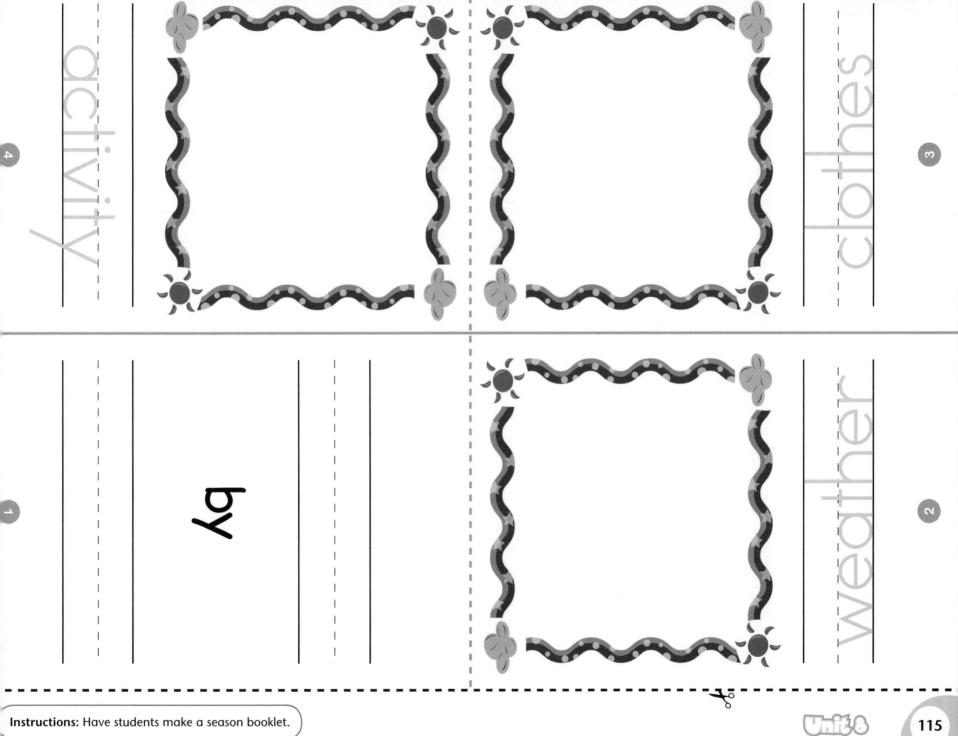

activity

4

clothes

3

by

1

weather

2

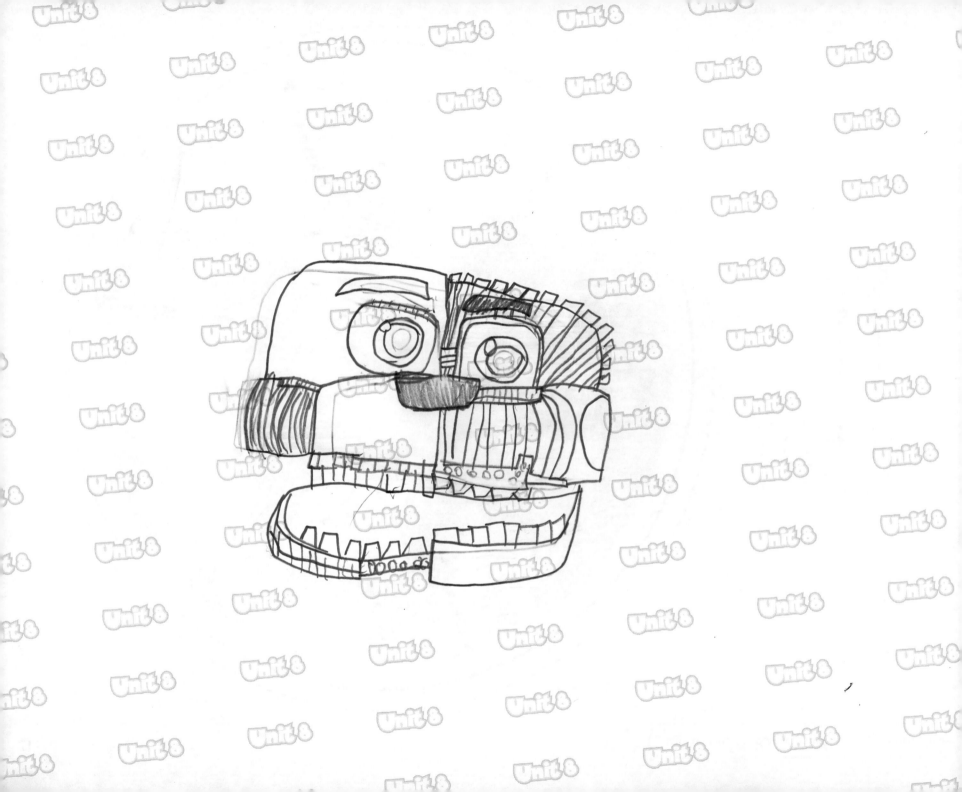

Write and circle.

Name: _____

Season	Hot or Cold	Activities
① Summer	_____ - - - - - - - - - - - _____	
② Autumn	_____ - - - - - - - - - - - _____	
③ Winter	_____ - - - - - - - - - - - _____	
④ Spring	_____ - - - - - - - - - - - _____	

Draw and complete.

winter	spring
summer	autumn

_____   _____

- - - - - - - - - - - - - - -   - - - - - - - - - - - - - - -

I _____ in _____ .

Unit 8

mouse

log

sun

frog

hat

house

cat

bun

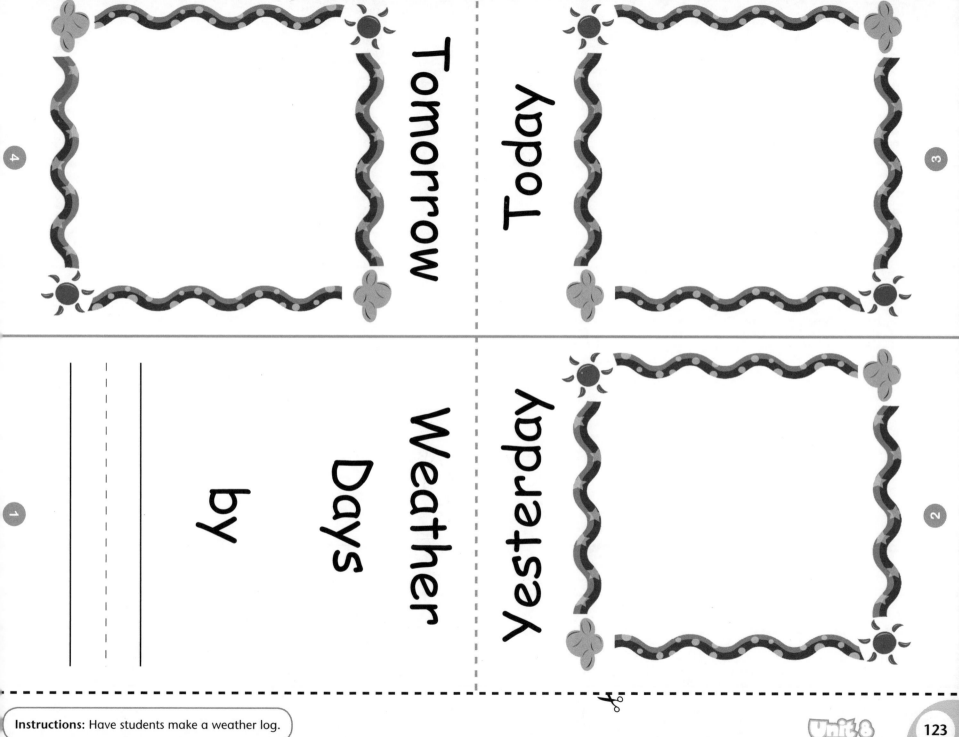

Tomorrow

4

Today

3

Weather
Days

by

_____
- - - - - - - -
_____

1

Yesterday

2

Unit 8

Instructions: Have students make a weather log.

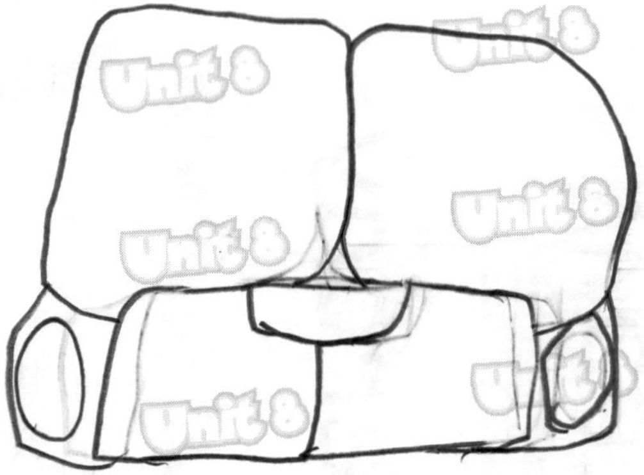

Read and complete.

Name: _____

December = 5 ☀ days   April = 10 ☀ days   July = 15 ☀ days

Sunny Days	December	April	July
20			
15			
10			
5			

Look and number.

Name: _____